CHI-TOWN: ENABLING GREATNESS

CHI-TOWN: ENABLING GREATNESS

JOHNNIE JAMES JONES III

This book is dedicated to the memories of Joyce Hunt and Barbara Peterson. To my cousins Andrea and Sharon, I must admit the hairpin in the electric socket incident that happened over fifty years ago was me – sorry you shared my punishment but I love you.

Contents

Introduction

When one spends over twenty years helping Chicago children and adolescents experience academic success while creating an inner confidence that makes college a realistic possibility, you begin to respect the unique journey of each.

What drives a person to reach out to others? What motivates an individual to work towards helping others succeed? What's in it for me? For some, it's the gratification of knowing that somehow they have made a difference.

By examining the work of Make A Difference Youth Foundation in Chicago, you will begin to appreciate the many challenges that students encounter during their journey towards adulthood.

To experience much in life helps one to realize that anything is possible.

I

WHERE'S DAD?

———————

Yesterday I was wearing jeans, but today it's shorts on a hot sunny day – while sitting on plastic. Someone thought it was a "good" idea to lose half your skin to save a stain. My sister's wearing a little skirt but is smart enough to sit still while I keep forgetting and occasionally swing my legs – until the plastic claims another piece of my skin. I hate to say it, but mom must have lost her mind when she covered all the furniture with plastic.

I'm guessing we're going on vacation since mom has the luggage by the door. I don't see dad and haven't seen him in a long time. I guess we will be meeting him somewhere after we leave. Hmmm, starting to understand this "plastic and skin" thing, as long as our legs are sticking to it, mom doesn't have to tell us to be still.

I can hear another train coming; I can't see it, but I can hear it rumbling over the big wall in front of the house. How do those trains get on the wall? One day I'm climbing that wall ... Boy, I hate when she screams my name like that. I'm small, but I'm not deaf. "Yes, mom." "No, I haven't moved." She never asks my sister those questions. But look at her, little miss pretty. Got her hands folded in her lap – just trying to make me look bad. "I said I haven't moved." "No ma'am, I'm not yelling at you, and you really don't need that belt ...". It's time to start crying; I need some tears ... come on tears. "No, I don't think you're playing with me ... I'm sorry mom". Don't know why she's crying; she's the one with the belt. Why is my sister telling mom it will be all right?? She must be trying to get me whooped!! Now the tears are flowing, I can't run because I'm stuck to this plastic. I'm a sitting duck, and this isn't going to end well.

I must be missing something. My sister and mom are hugging, and mom won't stop crying. What have I done? "Mom I'm sorry." Mom looked at me and said, "It's not your fault." Now I'm really confused. Another train and I can hear my friends outside cheering. They run down the street chasing the sound until it fades away. No cars come down our street, and that wall just goes forever. " Owww!!! She picked me up and pulled my skinny little legs off hot plastic. Why not just hit me with the belt!!! Oh, but little miss pretty gets to peel herself from the couch slowly. Not the iodine! I'm feeling a lot better – I have to learn to stop complaining!!! Mom, I didn't need that skin!!! "I'm willing to take my chance with the infection thing." The problem with being a toddler is they just don't speak my language. When I learn to talk, we are really going to discuss understanding body language and facial expressions. Like this expression means ... forget it; she still has that belt.

Now I have to get in the car on vinyl seats that have been baking in the sun all day. Can anyone say child abuse! Neighborhood kids think my skinless legs with red dye from that stinging disinfectant looks funny. Yeah just keep laughing. Yes, I'm about to get in that old hot car. "Keep laughing; it doesn't bother me at all." I can't cry. I can't let them see me cry. The handle is broken on my side so I can't roll my window down to get a little air. But look over there, my sister's window has a handle – "Hey sis, you enjoying that breeze, how about rolling that window down a little more so I get some air." Ooooh, so you're going to roll it up, so it's only open enough for you to get some air. Thanks, sis!!! Love ya! "No mom I'm not bothering my sister." "Hey ... that's not the truth; I'm sitting over here by the closed window on hot vinyl minding my own painful business".

Boy, I can't wait till I learn to talk. "Now how are you driving and reaching back trying to hit me with that belt?" Mom got skills, she hasn't missed me yet and still has her other hand on the steering wheel. I'm glad I'm so entertaining for my sister. Hope she don't hurt herself laughing at me getting my butt whooped while stuck to vinyl. "Stop"!!!! Oh God, the only word I know is going to get me in trouble. "No mom you don't have to pull the car over." "Stop telling mom to pull the car over ... I'm your brother".

"What exactly do you mean ... stop crying and clean my face, did you forget what's been happening during this ride?" "Hey look ... we're at Aunties house". I love visiting my uncle.

I wonder why we're headed to the basement with the luggage. I never knew there was furniture down there and a bunch of little rooms. The couch is right under a window, but all you can see is the bottom of the bushes and grass. But if I stand on the couch I can see the feet of people walking by. How cool is that? Gym shoes, church shoes, more church shoes, Owww! Excuse me, but no one said don't stand on the couch!! Why do you keep asking me questions when you know I can't talk yet? You can ask all the questions you want. BUT I STILL CAN'T TALK. Keep laughing sis.

I love this place. It's small but hidden. Just a couch and a chair in the living room, with a portable black and white TV, coffee table and empty magazine rack. The window over the TV is made of little frosted blocks, so you only see blurry objects go by. The kitchen looks like a play set with a tiny fridge, stove and sink all in a horseshoe around a table that sits three. The kitchen door leads to the stairs and looks like the only way in or out, but I still have more investigating to do on this place. "I'm not going to break anything ... you need to be watching my sister ... oops" ... Now why did they put that there??? I know, you told me to be careful. "Stop telling her you think I need another whooping" I'm starting to wonder about that girl. Why is mom crying again? She went from unpacking to crying.

Neither of the bedrooms has doors. They are connected by a little walkway on the opposite side of the kitchen. No bathroom??? What is in this extra closet with no light? Why is that string hanging from the ceiling – Too high for me to reach but not for little Miss Princess. Oh my God, this is the bathroom!!! No tub, just a tiny square room in the corner with a shower hidden behind a curtain facing a toilet and small porcelain sink. Guess this is home, but where is dad?

2

NEW BEGINNINGS

———————

We have been here a long time, I still haven't seen daddy, and mom always seems to be crying. My sister's only a year older than me but already helps mom cook. I finally learned to talk, but not much is said when mom gets home from work. My sister is always reading while I just like to stand on the couch and watch people go by – until I hear the door opening.

My sister goes to school while mom works. I get to stay upstairs with my uncle and aunt, usually playing with my plastic cowboys and indians. My uncle likes to walk me to the park located behind a big high school and let me watch the big boys play baseball. I want to play one day – if someone ever teaches me how. My uncle is retired, so we just sat together on the park bench until it was time to head home. I dreamed of one day having a baseball glove like the big boys and throwing that little white ball. I'm going to teach myself one day and be better than everyone else. I would close my eyes and imagine playing game after game with people cheering me on. But eventually, it was time to take the slow walk back home where we would be greeted by a cold glass of Kool-Aid that my aunt always left in the kitchen for us. My sister would be back from school and learning to sew with my aunt. But she never got to touch the big black Singer sewing machine with the racing car pedal that made it go. Sometimes they would be knitting or some other girly thing. But we men played with plastic cowboys and indians until my uncle eventually fell asleep in his chair.

Mom would come home with stacks of papers to grade – she was a teacher. Once she arrived, we would head down to the basement using the stairs behind the hallway door leading to our new home. Mom would always ask, "Did he behave?" and I could count on my uncle having my back ... But not my aunt! She gave a detailed description of everything I did – the woman missed her calling as a sports commentator. My uncle would sit and shake his head as my aunt read off the endless list. My mom would just stare at me while my sister smiled until the list finally came to an end. "You want me to get your belt mom?" By now you know who that was. My uncle would pat me on the head before I took the slow walk down the stairs with a smiley sister and an angry mom.

My mother would get her belt and sit it on the kitchen table next to a stack of student papers she had to grade. I sat quietly on the couch facing my mother while she graded her papers. My whooping would not take place until the last paper was graded. So I got to watch the belt and the stack of papers slowly dwindle to none.

The smaller the pile, the more tears would roll down my face. My sister would always seem happy about me getting a whooping but as the stack went down she would sit on her bed crying, knowing what was about to happen. I was a little renegade who refused to do what I was told. Then I would turn around, pull my pants down and shake my butt at my aunt while laughing. My uncle would warn me I was going to get in trouble, but I loved to show out. "This is going to hurt me a whole lot more than it hurts you" is what my mother would always say, while I was thinking, "then don't do it and nobody gets hurt." But I realized why she did it and afterward she went to her room and cried. One night she did not whoop me after grading her papers and told me to go to bed. For a strange moment, I felt deprived like I didn't get something I deserved. I heard her praying in her room for God to give her strength to continue and to help her with me. My sister went and laid down with my mom, while I laid in my room alone. I stopped terrorizing my aunt after that. I did not want to make mom cry again.

Eventually, I was old enough to go to school. I got to walk to school with my sister. She helped me straighten up my clothes and put my school supplies together. I never got the buttons right on my shirt and would always be one or two buttons off, but I didn't care because my sister would unbutton the shirt, show me how to line up the bottom button and make sure I tucked my shirt in my pants. I just hated when she licked her fingers and wiped something off my face. Then again, mom did that too – when she wasn't putting Vaseline all over my face making me shine like a new copper penny.

There were no school buses, so everyone walked. Crossing guards and patrol boys (who wore bright orange belts that buckled on their waist and crossed the chest) helped you get across each busy street. You only crossed the street where there was a crossing guard, and most of them were mean old ladies who enjoyed yelling at kids – they enjoyed their jobs. A few were very friendly and knew everyone's name. They all knew my sister and smiled when she came near. It didn't take long before they called us the good little girl with her bad little brother. I never saw a smile turn to a frown so fast, look at her smile – then look at me (growl). The way they looked at me, I realized that if my sister weren't there, I'd end up on a milk carton.

Kindergarten class had a big circle on the floor, lots of toys and a little place for us to put our coat and supplies. We would sit around the circle, and the teacher would ask us to cross our legs like an Indian. I was puzzled. None of my plastic Indians were in a sitting position. The other kids had attended pre-school and knew what to do and laughed at me. I didn't like school anymore. One chubby little kid kept making fun of me, and everyone would laugh so I put him on my list! Yes, I kept a list even in kindergarten, and when it came time to form a single file line to go to the bathroom, I grabbed a stick pin from the presentation board and waited for the right moment. As we marched along the wall to the bathroom, I poked chubby boy in the butt with the pin. He jumped like he was getting a rebound and screamed so loud it echoed through the halls. The first thing the teacher did was grab me and ask, "what did you do?"

Suspended from school in Kindergarten and being sent home.

They called my aunt and had two patrol boys walk me home. I ran to my uncle's room and asked him to take me to the park, but for the first time he yelled at me and sent me to the back room to lay down until my mother got there. My aunt wouldn't even look at me. When mom got there, she dropped her papers, grabbed me and took me down the stairs. Mom was a teacher and did not appreciate bad behavior in school – especially from her kids (that would be me since my sister was an angel). I got my worst whooping that night and my sister held me until I fell asleep while saying over and over "please learn to be good."

I got up to go to school in the morning, and my mother told me I was banned from school for a week, so I had to stay with my aunt and uncle. When school was out, I went to play with my friends, but they stood inside the screen doors and said their parents wouldn't let them play with me because I'm too bad. No one could play with me anymore. I went home crying, so my uncle took me out and bought me toy soldiers and a coloring book. I loved to color and then draw the things I colored. I started setting up my toy soldiers in battle scenes all over the house while starting to retreat into my own little world. My mother often took us to the library to let us pick out books and to watch puppet shows, so my world became my toy soldiers and my books. The other kids were coloring and learning their letters while I already could read. When I went back to school kids looked at me funny and would not say much to me; one teacher told a kid, "Stay away from him because he's crazy."

I didn't get in trouble at school anymore because I knew no one wanted me around, so I stayed to myself until my sister picked me up to walk home from school. She played with my soldiers with me and read with me and became my only friend. One day one of my old friends from the block came by, his parents said it was okay for him to visit me. He became my best friend. He would walk with my sister and me to and from school. Eventually, all the kids were allowed to play with me again, but he was still my best friend. My mother was so happy that I had friends again and invited them all to my first birthday party. My aunt said we could have the party upstairs, but I was not ashamed of living in a basement. I showed all my friends how to stand on the couch and watch the feet go by out the front window – they all thought it was so cool.

I loved my books and got cowboy and war books to get ideas for my legion of plastic people. My uncle and mom would buy me the bags with 100 pieces, and I created war reenactments everywhere. That's when I found out my uncle served in the military. He took me to his room and showed me all the black and white photos of him and my aunt. I made the mistake of saying, "Auntie used to look good" which was greeted by a slap on the head. He told me so many stories as we went from one photo album to another. My uncle was a soldier!

3

ON THE MOVE AGAIN

Once you establish a reputation, you never lose it. As I moved on to another grade, my teacher had me decorate the hall board with my drawings. I took it serious and was proud when people complimented my board. One of my classmates got jealous of the attention I was getting and did the unthinkable. He stood next to the board while I was drawing and screamed as loud as he could while yelling that I stuck him with a pin, another boy said he saw me do it. My past had caught up with me, and everyone believed them.

The principal rushed out her office and yanked me from the chair I was standing in by my ear and dragged me to her office. I screamed in pain as she called me an evil little boy. She left me on the front office bench while she called my mother and the police. Then she grabbed me again by my ear and dragged me into her office. I begged her to let go of my ear, when she got mad and slapped me. The slap caused me to lose my balance, slam into a wall, and fall to the floor. When the principal realized what she had done, the real nightmare began. She started throwing things from her desk and yelling "what are you doing?" teachers ran into her office and held me to the floor yelling, "hurry and get the police." My mother came to the school to get me, and they said I was being expelled from the school and needed to transfer to a school for violent kids. My mother was so embarrassed and ashamed. When we got home I got a whooping, but I didn't cry from the pain, I cried because no one believed me – no one but my sister. I was sent to see a psychiatrist, but the boys later admitted I never stuck anyone. And none of the kids believed that I went crazy in the principal's office. They felt bad they had set me up. But it was done, and now my mom would have to move to a new neighborhood so I could go to a different school.

Sitting on the couch again with my sister as luggage was lined up by the door. This time mom is not packing. She just sat at the kitchen table with her head down, occasionally looking our way as we sat quietly with our hands folded in our laps. I swung my little legs back and forth while my sister was completely motionless with her legs crossed, looking straight ahead. "Stop that … you're getting on my nerve". It looks like mom was not happy with me, but I smiled, while my sister stared at me before pinching my hand. I retaliated by kicking her … but guess who got caught? "Why did you do that? Why would you kick her and she did absolutely nothing to you?" Here we go again!

It was time for another car ride with luggage in the trunk and a window that won't roll down. Riding through one neighborhood after another and although the scenery seems to change, all the people look the same – they just seemed to get older. There were brick houses surrounded by metal chain fences and dirt where grass used to grow. We drove through an alley which led to a parking lot behind matching two-floor buildings. This place was amazing! I stood in the living room before running to the kitchen, then down the stairway to the basement. Back up the stairs to another stairway that led to three bedrooms. "Which room is mine?" – No more living in a basement.

A playground across the street next to the biggest school I had ever seen. Playgrounds did not have grass, just white gravel everywhere. Tall metal sliding boards, monkey bars, and swings all a short walk from home. I wondered if I would be attending the school by the park. Soon I would find out that the school across the street was somehow out of the district, meaning my sister and I would have to walk a mile to our new school.

Candy stores with arcade games, liquor stores, beauty shops and churches everywhere. Maybe a coincidence, but chicken places near almost every big church: Churches Chicken, Kentucky Fried Chicken, Chicken Unlimited, to name a few. Shut down stores were turned into churches, old mechanic shops were churches, and churches were next door to churches. We had moved to the neighborhood of religion, chicken, and fabulous hair.

Each time we walked home from school, we stopped by the candy store for penny candy and potato chips with hot sauce – for an extra two cents they would open your bag of chips, add hot sauce and shake them up. My sister would get a pickle with a peppermint stick in the middle while I would put twelve cents in the comic book machine to add to my collection. Comic books intrigued me because of the artwork. The stories were great, but my interest was in being able to draw the superheroes in murals. Each mural was a combination of fight scenes from different comic books. My collection of comics had reached the thousands!

One day I got home with a new comic but could not find my other comic books or drawings. My sister and I searched everywhere and eventually decided to ask my parents when they got home. My mother had remarried, and her new husband moved in with us.

My mother got home from work but had no idea where my comics had gone. When my stepfather got home, he said he threw them all out because he considered them stupid books for stupid people. He said if I wanted to read then I should read a real book. I ran to the alley to look for my books, but he said the garbage man had already picked them up. I sat in the parking lot crying until he grabbed me and dragged me into the house. I was told never to bring another comic book into his house. I stopped drawing and reading all books. I retreated to my new world of GI Joe action figures and Bonanza action figures. My mother got me new action figures with accessories to add to my growing collection.

I came home after school one day to find the heads ripped off my Bonanza figures and their arm springs stretched until their arms and legs dangled. I spent weeks trying to put the heads back on and fix their arms and legs until my stepfather threw them all out. I grew tired of being called stupid and a retard while my frustrations many times led to me making comments that came with significant consequences. Many times being picked up by my neck and repeatedly punched. Always ending in, "you better not tell your mother," so I always told my mother that some bullies in the neighborhood beat me up again. One day my sister caught one of my beatings and called the police. The police came but did nothing but joke with my stepfather about keeping kids in line. My sister also told my mother, and she rarely left me alone around my stepfather again.

After my mother's marriage, we changed churches and went to church almost every day of the week. Bible study, choir rehearsals, Usher practice, all day Sundays for morning service, afternoon service and Christian Youth Fellowship in the evening. But we loved church and made a lot of friends. We all sat together when our parents sat in the choir stand, and we passed notes as well as played games on paper – like connecting dots to form boxes.

One day I fell asleep during church, and my stepfather saw me from the choir stand. He came out the choir stand, woke me up and walked me to the men's bathroom where he beat my head on a sink yelling at me for disrespecting God's house. I fell to the floor while he cleaned the blood from the sink and told me to go home and change clothes. He made me walk home so I would learn to stay awake. I did not have a key so I crawled behind some bushes and went to sleep scared of what would happen when he got home.

My mother was worried about the neighborhood since I was regularly being beaten and decided to move. She had no idea that her husband was the one doing the beating. We moved to a neighborhood with very few Black families.

This time we moved into a house with a big yard, three bedrooms, a living room, full basement and a "sit down" kitchen. There was a huge park around the corner with tennis courts, volleyball courts, basketball courts and baseball fields. The park was filled with baseball teams of all ages, and I could imagine myself one day in a uniform playing baseball.

The baseball league did not have open registration; they had try-outs. On tryout day each person was given a number that was pinned to their back. Coaches hit balls to players and threw pitches to them while other coaches stood with clipboards taking notes. I didn't hit one ball, couldn't catch or throw the ball but was having so much fun. At the end of tryouts, the coaches went into a little building in the park and held a player draft. After the draft was over, the coaches taped the names of each team – and the players selected – on the window of the building. Not everyone got selected so they would have to wait for the next year to try again. I was not selected while all the other guys living on my block were drafted. After school, I would watch them practice and also attend their games. One of my neighbors offered to teach me to play. He took me to the rear of a grocery store and drew a box on the wall. We went to the store and bought white "major league" brand rubber balls – those were the only balls we used. The box represented the strike zone, and he threw me pitches while teaching me to hold the bat and swing. We also went to the park, and he would hit balls to me and show me how to catch balls on the ground and in the air. I only had a little plastic base-ball glove that came with a little red ball. He had a real leather glove but was left handed so I could not use it. My hand would hurt every time I caught the ball, and eventually, the ball tore up the glove. I told my mother I needed a real baseball glove, so she ordered me one from the Sears catalog.

The next year I went to tryouts with my new baseball glove, and at the end of the day, I saw my name listed with a team called the Rockets. It was the greatest day of my life. While everyone else was just checking to see what team they were on, I was just excited to be on a team!

League rules did not force coaches to let all players play in a game. You had to earn playing time during practice. Most guys on the bench were just happy to have a uniform and worked hard in practice in hopes of getting a bat or chance to spend an inning in the field. My first year on the team I did not get in one single game, but I was the first and last person in practice. But the next year most of the guys moved up to the next age group while I had one more year left. I was given a chance to play in games and was so excited when I got my first hit that I forgot to run to first base. I stood in the batter's box and watched them throw me out from the outfield. Everyone laughed at me, but I was still excited that I was in the lineup and actually hit the ball. My coach looked at me and smiled, "Did you enjoy how that one looked ... it looks even better when you're standing on a base."

I was playing left field and someone hit the ball my way, I heard the crowd, I heard my coach, I got so excited that I tripped over my foot and started falling to the ground when the ball "happened" to drop in my glove. I didn't realize the ball was in my glove and laid on the ground in embarrassment. I didn't want to raise my head until the coach ran over and patted me on the back and said great catch. He asked if I were okay and everyone was cheering. He took me out the game because he thought I was hurt and everyone came by the bench to congratulate me on a great catch. We didn't have dugouts, just a long board held up by two round metal bars on each side of a large metal backstop. I couldn't wait to get home and tell my mom, but I had to wait for the game to end.

The Rockets were the joke of the league and had never won a game. But during my last year on the team, the name was changed to the Mets, and we had become a pretty good team. We made it to the playoffs, but my family was going on vacation, so I missed the playoffs. My last year in that age group, my first year as a starter and I had to leave on vacation.

It took two years to make it back as a starter. The schedule was changed to include games on Sundays. In my house, we were not allowed to do anything on Sunday outside of attending church. The last game of the season was on a Sunday, and we needed to win to make the playoffs. My stepfather said I could not play so I hid my uniform and glove in front of the house in a bag behind the bushes. I went to church with my family then later snuck out and took public transportation back home. I was not allowed to have a key to the house, so I changed into my uniform in the back yard. That's when I realized I forgot my baseball socks and cleats. But I ran to the park in my baseball uniform, black socks, and dress shoes. When I got to the park the game had started and my team cheered when they saw me. The coach called timeout and was putting me in the game when he saw my dress shoes. He was about to have one of the players on the bench give me his shoes, but I refused to let the guy be embarrassed (I had my glove and parts of my uniform taken in the past for starters and knew how embarrassing that was). People laughed at my black socks and dress shoes until I ended the game with a running catch in center field to send us to the playoffs.

I was so excited to tell my mother that I ran in the house in my uniform (forgetting I was told not to play baseball on Sunday) and my stepfather gave me one of my worst beatings ever (as well as my mother for trying to stop him). I was banned from playing any more baseball that year. The greatest day of my life quickly turned into the worst day of my life as my mother took a beating because of me. Afterward, my stepfather rushed back to church because the choir had to sing at another church.

4

LEARN TO RUN

———————

Being one of a handful of Black families in the neighborhood, we stuck together to keep from being attacked. One day while playing in my yard, my neighbor and his friends came by and took my friend and me to his garage, tied us up and locked the door. They promised to release us if we stayed quiet until they got back. My mother got worried when she could not find me and called the police. We could hear the police next door, and my mother was crying. I called for my mother, and the police came over and released us. The officers refused to press charges against the kids that tied us up because they insisted that it was just boys being boys.

Another day, while playing in my yard, the neighborhood white guys asked if we wanted to have a pebble fight in the alley. They explained the game, and we agreed to play. The game was to begin in the middle of the alley, and anyone hit by a pebble was out. My friends and I gathered small stones and walked through the alley looking for the other guys. They showed up at one end of the alley in hockey equipment with bricks and started throwing them at us. We ran from gate to gate trying to find an unlocked one to get out of the alley until we got to one friend's yard. We hid on the side of the garage until we thought they had left. I went to the gate to see if they had left and was hit in the eye by a brick. I was knocked unconscious, and my friends carried me home. They tried to sneak me in the house, but my mother screamed when she saw the blood all over my face and clothes. She drove me to the local hospital where I received stitches and a patch to cover the eye. I lost vision in that eye, and the doctor said I would never regain full vision again – I never did.

The next baseball season came, and I could not see the ball. I became terrified when batting or in the field since I could not see the ball until it was close to me. Eventually, I started closing one eye and trying to estimate where the ball was going until I ran down a fly ball only to have it hit me directly in the face. It soon became apparent that I was scared of the ball and my baseball days were over. I loved the game and kept trying to play, but all I could see was a blur and then a ball at the last second.

After my last year of playing baseball, the league president asked me why I started to fear the ball. When he found out what happened, he allowed me to become the league's youngest coach at 16 years old. The league could not afford uniforms for my new team, so I went to the owner of a local glass block company to try and get him to sponsor team uniforms. When I got to the glass block company, the office workers laughed at me and felt I was running a scam. As I was leaving, the owner came out of his office and said he would buy the uniforms.

Now I needed to assemble a team. Each year the makeup of the neighborhood changed as white families moved out and Black families began to move in. The community comprised mainly of single family brick homes and a few frame homes with aluminum siding. Many of the newer kids had not participated in organized sports, so most coaches ignored them. Those kids became my main recruits. My recruiting grounds centered around two elementary schools that were located within walking distance of the park.

I once attended one of those elementary schools when it was a one-floor building with kindergarten through sixth grade. Eventually, mobile units were brought in to allow classrooms for a sixth and seventh grade – while they built a new school that would have room for students through the eighth grade.

I became a high school student coaching two teams while enjoying being a teenager. During those days you were able to count on a house party almost every weekend in someone's basement. Some parties where quarter parties (25 cents admission fee), and some were waistline parties that you got charged by the inch (your waistline). One Saturday evening, I left one of those parties with a friend who was about to walk home through the park by herself.

As we walked through the open field under the park lights, we laughed and talked about the party until I was suddenly put in a headlock by someone who came up behind me. Another guy put a gun to my head and let me know I was in big trouble. My friend happened to be a gang leader's girlfriend. It did not look good for me to be with her alone in the park at night. We were both forced to sit on a park bench while they sent someone to get him. Those were the days without cell phones, so we sat on a park bench beside rusted old volleyball courts waiting to die.

The concrete walking paths were dimly lit so you could see shadowy images of individuals as they slowly approached. I saw those images approaching with one guy giving me a look of confusion. He grabbed me off the bench and said to walk with him as if we knew each other. He asked me why I was with his woman and I explained that we were at a party earlier, and I was trying to make sure she got home safely since she was walking through the park alone. He walked me back to the bench and asked the guys if they knew who I was. Before they could answer, he said, "This is my little brother's baseball coach. He keeps my brother out of trouble." He told them to let me go and then looked at me and said, "Be careful heading home … it's dangerous in the park at night". They laughed as I tried to get home "alive" as soon as possible.

5

WHAT'S NEXT

———————

My last year of high school and I was still coaching baseball without any plans for my future until my stepfather said I was too stupid for any college to accept me. My sister was attending a good university and planning to attend medical school. So I was determined to prove that I could get in college. I missed the application deadline for the University of Illinois, and they mailed back my application and fee. I was called in to meet with admissions at the engineering school where I applied. That is when I was shown the letter of reference from my high school counselor. The letter recommended that the school not accept me and said I was not capable of graduating from a college. Because of the recommendation letter, I was challenged to take honors calculus and make straight A's to be accepted by the university.

The first half of the final semester I received an A in calculus and went into finals of my last term with an A. When the final exam was passed out, I smiled but noticed a close friend had turned his test over and had tears in his eyes. He was a baseball player and needed to pass calculus to graduate and receive a baseball scholarship. There was no way he was passing so I took his test paper and answered the questions for him. He rewrote the solutions in his handwriting while I began to start on my test. The exam had ended before I had made it through half the test. At that point, I realized I had blown my opportunity to attend the engineering school.

I immediately applied to DePaul University and prayed I got accepted to a college – unlike my step father's prediction. Word got out that I failed my calculus final and teachers got on me for blowing my opportunity to attend a top engineering school. The calculus teacher asked my friend and I to explain how he got an A on the exam after flunking the class the entire term while I received an F on the exam after carrying an A the entire term. Instead of failing both of us for cheating, I received a D for the class, and he was allowed to pass the class and graduate. The school informed my parents and my stepfather enjoyed telling me I would never amount to anything. I began to think he was right.

But, I received a letter of acceptance from DePaul University right before graduation and planned to pursue a career in law when a letter of acceptance came in from the engineering school. I showed everyone at my high school and could not wait to show my stepfather. When I heard him coming in the back door, I handed him my letters of acceptance with a smile. That's when

I noticed his hand forming a fist and when he got to the top of the stairs he first walked by me then reached back and punched me in the face. I laid at the bottom of the basement stairs when I heard him running down the stairs and then felt his shoe repeatedly striking my side. I looked up as he stood over me with both hands clenched in a fist. He stomped on me then walked back up the stairs. Beneath the pain was a sense of gratification that I had proved I wasn't stupid.

While attending college, I was still coaching and brought my players to the campus to practice on the school's baseball field and see the rest of the campus in hopes of encouraging them to think beyond baseball. Each weekend I would drive to Northern Illinois University to visit a young lady I had been dating since seventh grade. One weekend I could not reach her to verify that I was coming. When I arrived on campus, the students in the dorm knew me so they let me go straight up to her room. Her door was partially open so I pushed it open and saw her kissing another guy. She looked at me and said, "Now you know." The guy laughed as I walked out the room and headed out the dorm to my car. To explain the pain I felt that day is impossible. I drove back to my dorm and waited until morning to go to an Army recruiting center and enlist to leave immediately. I went home to tell my family and friends that I was headed to the military and shipped off soon after that.

6

BE ALL I CAN BE

———

I was headed to basic training and still could not clear my mind of that night in the dorm. I pictured the smile of a beautiful young lady I took on two proms and grew to love over seven great years. Her name and her soft voice echoed through my mind, and nothing else seemed to matter. Day after day I went through training while my mind was still stuck in the past that was impossible to accept as over. I received a letter apologizing for how our relationship ended and asked that I take care of myself. The letter only reminded me how much I really missed her in my life. She ended the letter with the little smiley face that she always drew by her name but no longer with the words "I love you." I went to my knees and prayed that the pain would someday go away.

Every night I prayed after training. One night a Hispanic soldier

———

asked if he could pray with me. After a while, my entire barracks joined me in prayer. During one evening of prayer, a big guy from Kentucky asked to sing a song. His tenor voice hit notes that sent chills through your body as you could feel the presence of the Lord.

No matter who I met while in the military, my mind remained on the one I lost. One day I met a young lady from my home state and we loved just to sit and talk. But she was white; the other soldiers mistook two friends as a Black guy dating a White woman. Things got real ugly as guys started telling me to stick to my race. She was a farm girl from southern Illinois and terrified of the aggressive guys that felt any female in the military was there to find a man. I introduced her to a good friend and before I knew it they were engaged.

Eventually, I met someone and got married. After my first son was born, I decided it was time to go back to school and make a real life for my family. When my time in the military ended, I had to decide if I was going to reenlist or go back home to college. I was broke and did not have the money to return home but did not want to tell my mother. One of my aunts called me to find out when I would be back from the Army and I let her know I was planning to reenlist. She immediately wired me money to move and get my family situated. She told me that she believed in me and that meant the world to me. I returned to the engineering school and moved into an apartment in the back of a photography studio. Eventually, I became a single parent of two boys and was even more determined to graduate.

One software development position after another caused me to change my focus to career while my mother continued to push the importance of a college degree. I returned to school but decided to transfer to a different university and pursue software development and mathematics.

During my final semester of college, I was added to the list of graduates and sent out graduation announcements. My mother was extremely proud until the day I received a letter that I would not be graduating. I was informed that I failed a final in a major class and was given a D for the semester which prevented me from being eligible for graduation. I did not understand since all my finals were a breeze. One professor insisted that I did not turn in all the pages to his final exam when I knew I did. I met with the dean but was informed that it was my word against a tenured professor.

The Dean spoke with other students in the class (there were less than ten students in the class), and each one told the Dean that I turned in my test – but the professor insisted I did not and he would not change my grade. I was devastated and decided I would never go back to school. But the Dean offered to allow me to take a class at no charge over the summer and graduate during the fall ceremony. I did it for my mother but refused to sign up for the fall ceremony. When I passed the class over the summer, my mother called me and said that I should not allow anyone to take away something that I had earned. I signed up for the fall graduation ceremony, and it was one of the greatest days of my life as my mother, sister, brother and both sons attended.

7

TIME TO MAKE A DIFFERENCE

———————

I never stopped coaching baseball but grew concerned that the boys were cheered while playing sports but forgotten when they were too old to play. Many could not read, write or put together a simple sentence. One young man I always thought about was as talented as they come but would be dropped off by drug dealers at practice and games wearing multiple pagers. I wanted to find a way to help those young men develop a plan for life beyond baseball, but the big question was "how?"

The supervisor at the park I coached in asked that some coaches sit on the park's advisory board to help plan park activities. I volunteered and spent each month in a big two hour argument called an advisory board meeting. Nothing was ever accomplished and at the end, they would just schedule the next meeting. During one meeting they began their usual arguing and I yelled, "I have had enough of this nonsense and am going to start my own organization that will do something for the youth." The head of the advisory board mocked me and asked, "So what are you going to call your organization?" I blurted the first thing that came to mind, "Make A Difference Youth Foundation ... because I'm going to make a difference". They laughed as I left the room, except two ladies and one man that followed me outside and said, "Let's do this".

I sat and spoke with my brother-in-law who was a high school student and told him my plans for helping high school students get into college. He got a bunch of his friends together and we held our first meeting in a football locker room with the two ladies and one guy from the park advisory board. We met each Tuesday evening and the group continued to grow. One evening I asked all the students to come up with a name for their college bound group. One young lady recommended TFANT. Then explained further, "Teens For A New Tomorrow". That became the name.

We decided to focus on preparing for college and helping in the community. These initiatives led to a different community service project every weekend. We wanted to do something big that would have a major impact on how the students felt about college — something that would show them that college wasn't just for those smart people, but for everyone with a dream. We decided to plan a college trip to colleges that vary in size, public as well as private and include Historical Black Colleges and Universities. It was the 90's and an unheard of undertaking, especially for an inner city group of young Black students. We knew that for the organization to succeed and grow, this trip had to happen. The schools and neighborhoods said it could never be done and gave every possible reason for failure, but I was determined and on a mission. Some parents and coaches from the baseball league joined in to help plan the trip. The big question, "where do we get the money?"

The city of Chicago was celebrating NBA championships and a new fundraising opportunity was born, the Scottie Pippen candy bar. We decided to see how many we could sell while allowing the students to plan the trip, which colleges we would visit, where we would stay each night and the transportation. We came up with a budget of expenses and the candy bars were consistently selling out. We kept ordering more and were becoming one of the top sellers in the city of that candy bar. We started booking tours at the colleges and putting deposits on hotels. We were pushing for enough to rent a coach bus but it wasn't looking good.

We called a parent meeting and explained that we could not raise enough for a coach bus but could afford to rent vans and drive. This was the turning point of the trip and the organization. A group of parents felt the trip should be canceled because driving vans would be too dangerous, while a second group was in agreement to do the trip with vans. It became more then a disagreement, it led to a protest and one group demanding the trip be canceled as they pulled their kids from the group.

The trip became more complicated since we planned to include two young baseball teams on the trip to play games scheduled at each city by various plants owned by the company I worked at (a container company). The purpose of the young baseball teams was to get young children exposed to college while doing something they enjoyed. The entire trip seemed in jeopardy as parent groups pressured other parents not to let their kids participate while protesting and interrupting our meetings. A group of parents, coaches and teachers volunteered to be drivers and the trip was on.

The day we met to leave from the park there was a huge protest group that planned to block the vehicles from leaving while yelling at the parents for allowing their kids to participate, but we drove off and the ten day college trip began. Since no one had cell phones, we put walkie talkies in each van and gave drivers emergency signal instructions in case they needed to pull over. After months of planning and fundraising we were on the road.

No one knew that I had quit my job the day before the trip – because of an incident at work. My company had helped plan the trip and bought a bunch of Scottie Pippen candy bars, but a confrontation occurred that caused me to make a career decision without disrupting the trip. I had been promoted at my company, and my team was introduced to our new manager who was brought in from Canada. When I was called into his office for my initial one on one meeting, he informed me that he canceled my promotion. He said he did not like people on his team promoted before he got a chance to see them perform – yet no other promotions on his team were canceled but mine. So I told him I needed to get something off my desk, I left his office and wrote a simple note on a small piece of paper, "I Quit". I placed it on his desk and never returned to the company. I did not tell anyone and the next day I was driving a van on the college trip. I was hired by a company as a consultant while on the trip to begin when I returned to Chicago.

Our first night of a ten day trip was a display of immaturity by kids who had never stayed in a hotel. Students were running up and down hallways, knocking on people's doors and hiding, having ice cube fights and completely disrespecting the hotel as well as its guest. I requested and was given a conference room and everyone was introduced to my "angry side". The message was simple; we would head back to Chicago and cancel the trip if I saw anyone in the halls, heard a voice or a sound. I had them march to the front desk and apologize to the hotel staff and go straight to bed. We never had another incident the entire trip. The next morning when I got up, all the students were already up, had their luggage packed and loaded in the back of the vans. They even had breakfast sitting at a table for me with coffee and orange juice. Before we left each morning, we held hands and prayed to give thanks to God for another day of life and for continuing to watch over us during our travels.

We visited two to three colleges a day while sleeping in a hotel each evening, then took a different route back to Chicago so we could visit different schools on the way back. The two baseball teams we brought wore Chicago White Sox uniforms and the high school students would cheer them on when they returned from their college trips. The teams they played setup picnics for us after the games had completed. We took both teams on walking tours of college campuses when they were not playing.

Half way through the trip our lead van began to speed. Everyone sped to keep up with him, and we were pulled over by a group of highway patrol cars. One trooper said, "This trip is over." I got out my van and asked the troopers if we could talk for a moment. The troopers and I walked away from the vans, and I first apologized for our reckless behavior by speeding and explained to them the significance of the trip. I asked them to hold me responsible and arrest me, but to please allow the kids to continue a journey of a lifetime. I handed them my driver's license and told them I understand and accept whatever they decide to do with me but to please not punish the kids for the bad decision of adults who were to blame for allowing it to happen. The ranking officer told me to keep my license and have a safe trip. He asked me to keep the speed down and that they would escort us to the state border. There was not any speeding again the entire trip.

As we drove to our hotel we found out it was one young lady's birthday so we picked up a birthday cake when we stopped for gas then pulled into a rest area and threw her a surprise birthday party. We all sang happy birthday and ate cake before getting back on the road.

The day we returned to Chicago we were greeted by many of the kids whose parents did not allow them to attend. The kids and parents who attended the trip could not stop talking about the ten days of colleges, amusement parks (we had special reservations at six flags over Georgia) and baseball games. None of the protesting parents were at the park when we returned but many contacted me later asking to be a part of the next trip regardless of how we traveled. We traveled to colleges throughout the state after the trip and our group continued to grow.

8

CITY POLITICS

———————

TFANT students met each Tuesday at 7 pm in the football stadium locker room that was used by the Chicago Park District as a field house for park activities. During one meeting we were informed by the park supervisor that the locker room was being shut down to meetings and the park district would no longer be maintaining a facility in the park. The students asked if it were too late to stop the shutdown, so I wrote a letter to the ward alderman to request that the facility remain open.

I received a reply letter from the alderman stating that it was out of the ward's hands and that nothing could be done. The letter ended by wishing the group and I well in our future endeavors. When I informed the students, they asked me to contact a local investigative reporter that had his own show on local issues called

———————

"Walter's Perspective." The reporter followed up with the alderman's office and was told by the alderman that she knew nothing about my organization and had never heard of me. The interview resulted in the reporter's staff contacting me to find out if I had proof of speaking to the alderman. I faxed them a copy of the letter I received from the alderman "on city hall letterhead." After they had received the fax, a camera crew was sent to our student's meeting. They interviewed students while documenting their academic and civic accomplishments. Then it happened! Commercials of the students leading up to a new "perspective" focused on the group and the alderman.

As the segment was aired, it began with a focus on the students and their interviews. It then discussed the conversation with the alderman followed by showing the letter I received from the alderman on air with my name and the organization highlighted and circled. They called the alderman out for lying live on TV. Her office was livid and contacted me to let me know. I became the bad guy for trying to save a program that helped students improve themselves as well as assist others in need. The locker room shutdown was canceled.

The expenses of running the organization started to mount as the group continued to grow. I decided that we would have one major project before shutting down for good. Local elections were about to begin, so we started planning a citywide election for students to run for mayor and city council. The election was set up for students from each city ward to run for alderman of their ward and for any student in the city to run for mayor. We created a board of elections and voter registration rules. Then we solicited the assistance of a web design company (ANET) to develop an online voting system that would allow the registration of student voters as well as enable them to vote online during the election. All candidates had to obtain the signatures of students registered to vote in the election before being added to the ballot. Candidates could challenge the signatures of their competitors to our student board of elections.

On Election Day a Chicago newspaper mentioned our election in an article, and we opened our website for voting at the same time city polls opened for the actual election. Each registered voter was given a code to use to vote and the code was deleted after being used. The website displayed the vote totals for all candidates after the voter finished voting. The availability of election results caused candidates to go out and make sure their friends and neighbors voted and to ask who was winning the race. With 30 minutes left in the election, a TFANT student was winning the mayoral race by over 100 votes. She began to celebrate. Suddenly a huge number of votes started to come in. By the close of the polls, our student had been caught and passed by the eventual winner. We found out that the school that the winner attended was hosting a basketball game, and the principal took all the students to their school library after the game to vote.

During the planning of the election, we worked with the mayor's office to arrange for the winners to meet their actual alderman, the mayor and for the web company to be recognized for donating their time and resources to create, host and monitor the election. After the election, we were told that the web company would not be recognized, and the alderman did not have time to meet the students but that we could come to city hall for a picture with the mayor. That decision ended our relationship with the web company since we were not able to get the city to recognize their efforts as promised.

The big day arrived for the election winners to meet the mayor. As they arrived, we all met in the lobby until greeted by a lady from the mayor's office. Many more things had changed. All the kids' parents came but were told they would have to wait in the lobby while the students took a quick picture with the mayor. The kids and their parents were disappointed but still excited to meet the mayor. When we entered the room with the students the mayor's representative provided further instructions. No one was to ask the mayor any questions because he had a busy schedule for the day and could not be delayed. The mood in the room had changed when the mayor walked in. He congratulated the students on running successful campaigns and winning their election. He stopped and asked why their parents did not attend. One young man raised his hand and told the mayor that their parents were in the lobby. The mayor's representative interrupted and told everyone to line up for the picture. The mayor stopped her and asked the young man why the parents were in the lobby. The young man pointed at the lady and said, "She told them to stay in the lobby." The mayor sent someone to bring the parents in and said this was a time for each family to celebrate together.

When the parents entered the room, the mayor asked if anyone had questions for him. This confused everyone. The lady from the mayor's office gave a glaring look to the students, but the same young man raised his hand again. The young man asked the mayor why was he asking for questions when they were told not to ask him any questions. The mayor asked him who told them not to ask questions and the boy once again pointed at the lady. The mayor pulled up a seat and told the kids to rearrange the chairs in the room so they could all sit together and talk about whatever they like. Many questions were asked, and the mayor answered each one before everyone lined up for a group picture with the mayor. After the group picture, the student winner of the mayor's election mother asked the mayor if she could take a picture of her son, husband and the mayor together. The mayor said no. He called his photographer over and said he would rather take a picture that also included her. The mother thanked the mayor over and over as she stood proudly by her son, husband, and mayor. The mayor told me he would have the picture sent to me to give to the family.

An alderman came into the room to find out what was going on and was shocked he was not informed about the election. He asked to take a picture with the student who won the election in his ward. Then he went back and told the other aldermen. They all came in the room and took pictures with the students and the parents. The aldermen then took the students to the council chambers and let them sit in their chairs while the speaker had their names added to the official city council meeting notes. As we were preparing to leave the mayor asked me what I was planning to do next. I told him the election was our organization's farewell since we had run out of money to continue. He patted me on the back and said he would have his budget director call and help us get a grant to continue. I didn't know what to think, but the budget director did call and schedule an appointment with me the next day. We were given our first grant.

Since we finally had some money we decided to move from the locker room and rent an office for our meetings. We found a location that was boarded up but had a for lease sign. I called the owner and met him for a viewing with a few of my foundation board members. The place had one room with a huge hole in the middle of the floor leading straight to the basement. The bathroom was missing a sink, and toilet, and the front window was all boarded up since there was no glass. He had the nerve to ask, "So what do you think?" The owner was an older man who said he was willing to negotiate to get the property rented. I told him it would take a huge investment on our part to put in a floor, a bathroom and make the place safe. He asked me to make him an offer. I told him we would do the work on the property if our rent stayed at $200 a month for five years. The owner agreed and drew up a lease.

A contractor that I knew – and helped to get a computer for his business and his family – volunteered to do the work for free. He just needed certain materials and said he would donate the leftover materials from other projects he completed. In about a month the place looked brand new. The owner came by and was shocked at the renovation of the room and bathroom. After our first year, I received a call from an attorney who purchased the building from the owner. He voided our lease and asked us to leave in 60 days or sign a new lease for $800 a month (a $600 a month increase). I told him about our program, and he said he could not care less, either produce the money or get out.

As we began our search for a new location, we found the rent at each site was higher than we could afford. Suddenly we received a response to a grant we applied for to participate in a national program sponsored by General Colin Powell, People Magazine, Time Magazine, Gateway Computer and AOL called PowerUP – bridging the digital divide. Our acceptance into the program was contingent on us meeting facility requirements as outlined in the program guidelines. There were electrical power requirements, room size, wall and ceiling specifications. They gave us two weeks to respond with a location for the inspection.

I immediately called our new alderman and explained the situation. She had her staff start looking into possible locations. That night I went for pizza and noticed the place next to the pizza restaurant was for rent. I called the owners first thing in the morning. The owner was a retired school teacher who ran a daycare in the same building with her husband. She loved the idea of having an educational group in the building and gave me the keys while drawing up a lease. I immediately contacted the PowerUp program with an address and had an inspection scheduled in 30 days. Then I went to the office and opened the door.

The place was a former beauty shop with six sinks and plumbing on each wall. I sat on the floor in disbelief while wondering how I could transform that room into what was required in less than 30 days with limited funds. While sitting on the floor with my head in my hands, the father of a high school student I allowed to stay in our office after school each day stopped in to check on our new location. I sat in near tears as I explained what needed to be done in a short period. The man was a single parent of a young lady who requested to stay in our office each evening until her dad picked her up. He said he needed to get something out his car and came back with a pipe wrench. He explained that he was a plumber for over 30 years and that a good plumber could do wonders with a pipe wrench. He proceeded to remove every sink from the walls as well as all the pipes. He did not stop until both walls were bare of all pipes and sinks. When he finished, he told me as a single father of a young lady living in the city, that it's difficult not to worry about her safety after school. He said he did not worry knowing she was at our office where she also received help with her school work. He called it an honor to be able to do something for us in return. I called it a blessing.

I stopped by my neighbor's house the next day since he did contracting work on the side. He went to the office with me that night, reviewed the room requirements and said let's get started tonight. I had to tell him that I was not good with tools or working with my hands but I would follow whatever directions he gave. I used my personal credit cards to buy drywall and supplies at the hardware store, and we began putting up walls that night. He contacted other people to help, and the contractor who did our first office got us a free electrician to do the wall sockets. I exhausted my bank accounts and started paying the workers with my personal computers, power tools, and other personal items they would accept until I ran out of things to offer. All the workers quit with just one week before the inspection but my neighbor wrote me out an IOU to promise to pay him later. We worked every evening and put the final coat of paint on the wall the day before the inspection.

Inspection day arrived, and we were approved. The PowerUp program provided us with a full computer lab donated by Gateway computers, complete networking, printers from HP, and the internet through AOL. We received software and specialized programming that we offered to elementary and high school students. I called it the 30-day miracle. A year later we were named national PowerUp site of the year.

The miracle continued when the mother of one of our students – who worked for the FBI – informed us that the FBI was donating all their office furniture to nonprofits. She was able to get enough desks and cabinets for all the new donated computer equipment.

The college bound group continued to grow and was set up like a corporation with officers heading each organizational function. The student placed in charge of community service selected three initiatives for the group to pursue: painting senior citizen homes, volunteering at the Greater Food Depository and feeding the homeless through church and shelter programs.

Our students started meeting at 7 am on Saturdays to head to CHA (Chicago Housing Authority) senior housing to paint rooms and hallways. This project continued each weekend for months until the city privatized the painting and volunteers were no longer used. Julie and Sal headed volunteer painting efforts and would provide a list of rooms and hallways that we were assigned to paint. Residents could refuse to have their rooms painted, and one day there was a gentleman who did not want anyone in his room. As we gathered our supplies and began to separate into groups to paint rooms and hallways, he sat in his doorway watching us. He was polite and nodded his head in acknowledgment of each person who greeted him. But he quietly sat and watched as we worked. He left his doorway for a moment to play a record on an old phonograph. As the music played, one young lady began to sing while she painted. The gentleman looked shocked. He walked up to her and asked where she had learned the words to that song. The young lady explained that it was one of her grandfather's favorites and she used to sing it with him before he passed away. He looked at her and said his grand-children would sing the song with him until they got older and stopped visiting him. He began to cry and asked if it were too late to have us paint his room. As we painted his room, he and that young lady sang song after song together. She even began to visit him on days we were not painting.

During a briefing with the city on a grant we received, I noticed a scholarship given by the city and DePaul University to students for volunteer work. One of our students was planning to attend DePaul and was one of our biggest volunteers – as well as volunteer for every week we painted senior homes. She worked with the city director of the senior painting project volunteers and was awarded the scholarship by DePaul. An honor student who enjoyed serving her community was rewarded for her efforts and is now a graduate of DePaul University.

9

DETERMINED

The first student to join and recruit students for our college bound program attended our first ten day college tour. He fell in love with Grambling State University and that campus visit became a turning point in his life. Realizing that the tuition to attend Grambling was not an option, he found a way to attend by first establishing residency (moving to the city after graduation, finding a job and joining the National Guard). This young man worked his way through Grambling State University and became the organization's first male college graduate. He went on to receive a graduate degree and begin a career with Nike.

We once had a group of students we just referred to as the Whitney Young crew – a group of students from the top high school in Chicago. One was a freshman young lady who loved to take charge. She became the first freshman president for the college bound program and went on to become the only four-time president in the organization's history. She was a leader that others loved to follow who got things done. She learned to empower others at a young age to build a strong leadership team. She led a team of "students" who negotiated dinners at major hotels for 500 to over a thousand guests. One evening her team invited me to join them at a "food tasting" at one of the hotel restaurants. Her negotiations team had hotels doing presentations to win the bid to host our annual graduation dinner. It was no surprise that she completed a five-year program that included an MBA and went on to manage a negotiation team for a major company.

Our college bound group became known for its bright motivated young ladies. One of those young ladies was part of a group we called our "McAuley girls" – our first of many groups of students from Mother McAuley High School. That group was extraordinary in and out of the classroom as they led community service projects throughout the city each and every week. But one had the ability to organize and motivate students from schools throughout the Chicagoland area to plan college trips, special events and weekly community service projects – with multiple projects sometimes taking place on the same day. I received a call one day to turn on a national news broadcast and to my surprise there she was being interviewed as a scientist working on the Gulf oil spill.

There was a young man that represented everything that our organization stood for. He was a high school football star whose classroom achievements combined with his constant desire to help those in need led him to be selected as president of our college bound group. It was no surprise that his academics landed him a scholarship but he surprised many by starting a nonprofit in the town by his university to provide tutoring for younger students. An engineering student with a rigorous schedule found the time to get funding for a building to host his tutoring program. He went on to become one of our many graduates from Florida A&M University.

The holiday break for many college students begins with finding a ride home. One holiday break left one of our former students fighting for his life while never giving up on his dream. A car ride home to Chicago from Illinois State University ended in a tragic accident leaving each passenger fighting for their lives. But for one young man, the battle was also to get back to school. This young man suffered massive damage to his body which also resulted in his jaws being wired shut, yet he still communicated through pen and paper that he had to get back to school. That young man returned to Illinois State University with his jaws wired ready to continue working towards a degree. His determination and eventual graduation motivated and inspired many of our younger students (as well as his peers) to never give up on their dreams.

With all the stories from days gone past, there stands the story of a young man admired by his peers while presenting a smooth "pretty boy" image admired by young female students everywhere he went. He was a bright yet smooth young man who seemingly did everything right and had the world in the palm of his hands. No one knew where he lived but assumed he must have come from big money.

One evening we had an event that went longer then expected and lasted well into the late hours of the evening. All of the students had parents pick them up except this one young man. I offered to drive him home but he insisted on taking public transportation – which I could not allow at that hour for a high school student. He insisted that I not call his parents since they did not answer the phone after a certain hour. It did not make sense to me. He finally realized I was not going to let him go alone and for the first time the look of confidence was gone from his face.

As we walked to my car he explained that his parents did not have a phone and had people call one of the neighbors in their apartment buildings phone – that family did not like to be called after a certain time. He made a simple request if I gave him a ride that I let him off a few blocks from his home and keep my car lights out until he made it in his building. The young man lived in a crack house and had to make his way past crackheads and gang members without being seen. I sat in my car watching him maneuver his way home. Before he left the car, he asked that I never tell anyone. He said that he hated Chicago and would one day leave and never return. His reason for being in our college bound program was to escape Chicago through college. On the way to his house I listened to a childhood of fear and constant beatings by crackheads and gang members that eventually led to his streetwise savvy as a means of survival. He was not who many thought he was, but he learned to deal with his fear. He went on to graduate from college and became a teacher but never returned to Chicago.

10

INTEGRITY

———

Our city of Chicago community block grant was renewed each year since the year the mayor helped us receive our first grant. But this year was different. We were sent new guidelines by the city that required we eliminate all educational programs and implement more fun based programs that kids would enjoy. I was told that kids should not have to do school work once they left school so if I wanted to continue to receive funding that I must stop tutoring and college readiness programs. I refused, and we lost our funding. As we prepared to shut down our organization, the kids and parents sent letters to the mayor's office. I also sent him a letter thanking him for the many years of support but that I could not eliminate educational programs and would close down before going against the organization's mission. I was contacted by the mayor's office as well as the department that administered the grant. The mayor did not agree with forcing us to shut down all educational programming and had our city grant reinstated. He had the department work with our head of tutoring (a former student from our program who was now an assistant principal in the Chicago Public Schools) to develop performance measures for our programs.

TFANT continued to send every high school graduate to college, and the number of former TFANT students graduating from college continued to climb. Our high school students served as tutors for our after school program, and we decided to look into expanding our programs for elementary school students by providing a full day summer camp based on a theme that combined constant learning with a lot of fun activities. We met with other organizations that offered summer programs to learn how to get free lunches for campers and develop a plan for taking them on a trip each week. A proposal was presented to the mutual fund company I worked with and they approved funding to run the camp and only charge parents ten dollars a week which included lunch, snacks and a weekly trip. The theme was Cultural Awareness and campers studied different cultures each week and would later meet with representatives of various embassies. The camp went well and led to additional funding each year from the mutual fund parent company – Morgan Stanley.

With the OK to continue our college bound program we reached out to a college in Upper Peninsula Michigan – Michigan State University – to attempt a virtual tutoring program with their students serving as mentors through a special tutoring website. The university agreed to participate in the program, and they had quite a few students that volunteered as tutors. The program provided our students with free advanced tutoring in AP classes, calculus and Physics. As our relationship grew with the university, we began taking students on visits to their campus.

We had one student who participated in the tutoring program who had spent three years of high school in special education classes. He was told he was slow. His school ended special education classes and he had to take regular classes. He registered for a chemistry class and with the help of tutors received a B. He was amazed and beginning to feel confident that he could take regular classes and be successful. He even began believing he could succeed in college. The young man remembered a special program run over the summer to give students a second chance at being accepted to the university. It was closing in on the deadline to apply so he got all his paperwork in and asked his counselor for the required letter of recommendation.

Weeks went by and no letter from the counselor. A month went by, and I contacted the counselor to let her know that time was running out for the young man to be considered for the program. The counselor informed me that she would not be wasting her time writing a letter for a special education student who had zero chance of making it in college when she could be spending her time helping students with a future. One of our board members (a retired teacher) went to the school to meet with the counselor to try to get her to send the letter and just give the young man a chance. The counselor refused so I wrote a letter to the Chicago Board of Education explaining the situation and they immediately stepped in. The young man got his letter and was accepted to the university's summer program.

A high school math teacher who heard about our tutoring program and college bound program contacted me about some students she had worked with at her high school. She felt they were bright young men who underestimated their potential. I spoke to one of those young men, and he was determined to work with his hands and was assured a job when he graduated from high school. But the young man noticed we had a lot of "pretty girls" in the group. He later found out that those pretty faces were high academic students. He began challenging himself and ended up at Southern Illinois University where he later graduated with an electrical engineering degree and now works for Boeing.

Another one of our students loved Michigan Tech University but realized the tuition would be a challenge for her parents. Her parents were excited about the many scholarships she had been awarded although none were to Michigan Tech. I drove her father to the university and when we returned to Chicago he told me that his daughter was going to attend that university one way or another. He said he had never seen her light up with excitement as much as she did while on that campus. By the time school had started, that young lady had received scholarships to attend Michigan Tech – where she later graduated as a chemical engineer.

The relationship with Michigan Tech went even further when our students found out about a Native American tribe affiliated with the university. The Native American students did not have the advantages of visiting colleges like our students so they decided to come up with a program that they could work on with those students and college bound students from another state. They called it the Global Communications Project and used video conferencing equipment to plan a student run conference in Dallas at Southern Methodist University (SMU). The Native American students were able to utilize the conferencing equipment at Michigan Tech; our students used our recently purchased video conferencing equipment and the students in Dallas used their equipment. Students from each city worked together on teams to plan a weekend conference on college readiness via weekly live video conferences.

Our students took on the responsibility for raising money to fund the entire project which included the plane flights for the Native American students and their chaperons in Michigan, flights for students and chaperons in Chicago, hotel expenses and the costs of renting buildings at SMU. Through dances and bowling outings (as well as many donations) they raised the money and held one amazing seminar.

On the day our students were scheduled to fly from Chicago to Dallas, one of our students showed up to the airport without an ID. The students' parents insisted that they could get her back home to get her IDs and get back before the flight took off. Our lead chaperone waited for the young lady to return. The plane began to board, and the chaperone realized she could no longer wait on the student. By the time she got to the gate, the plane was leaving. One of the chaperones called me from the plane (I was in North Carolina at the time) to tell me our lead chaperone had been left. A flight attendant overheard the conversation and told the pilot. Suddenly I was talking to the pilot! He told me to call my chaperone and tell her he was headed back to get her. The pilot announced he was going to get a chaperone and the entire plane cheered. What a way to start a trip.

When everyone returned home from the conference in Dallas, we received a bill for extended charges from the hotel for thousands of dollars – but we had no money. I came in from North Carolina and found an envelope from the Chicago Community Trust in the foundation mailbox that contained a check from an anonymous donor for the exact amount that we owed the hotel. I showed the board members the hotel bill and the unexpected check. They simply said we are blessed!

II

GEMS BEGINNING TO SHINE

––––––––––––

Everyone is not cut out to work with nonprofits. While working for one firm I was asked if one of the corporate execs could work with our organization as part of the company's initiative to be more active in the community. The guy was a financial wizard and helped us in developing budget forecasts while monitoring our actual expenses against our budget. As more restricted grants came in he helped us to separate and track individual program budgets while tying them to our overall foundation budget. He was a tremendous asset. But he hated to see money spent on social programs and felt there should be a price on our services. He felt we should exclude those who could not pay. It got worst.

During the winter we experienced extremely high heating bills. He recommended that we turn down the heat during our after-school programs and have the kids keep their coats on so we could use less heat. His reasoning was that they weren't paying for services and probably didn't have heat in their homes anyway, so it wouldn't be something that they weren't accustomed to. He eventually quit the board when we spent money on Christmas toys for needy families. He considered it outside of the scope of the organization mission and a waste of money on kids who were used to not getting anything for Christmas anyway. That year the students and parents worked together to raise funds to buy and wrap a van full of toys. The students met to wrap and label gifts as boy gift and girl gift – most toys were purchased by the students. Then, we all met at 7 am on Christmas day and drove through financially challenged neighborhoods surprising children with gifts.

One of the great things about our program was that our students came from schools throughout the city and surrounding suburbs. Over time they developed permanent bonds that lasted past high school and college. Principals and teachers worked with us, and colleges began sending buses and paying our hotel fees to get our students to visit.

Many young people are driven by a life changing event. One of our former high school students had an uncle accused of a crime he did not commit. He was unable to afford an attorney and was appointed one by the courts. The attorney convinced him to plead guilty to the crime because he did not have a criminal record and would not receive jail time while if he were convicted, he could spend a long time in prison. The fear of prison led her uncle to follow the attorney's advice, and he was sent straight to jail.

This high school student told me that she planned to become a public defender someday and give a fighting chance to those without the ability to pay for legal representation. While attending law school, her moot court team finished first place in the American Bar Association Mock Trial Competition by defeating the back-to-back champion Harvard University. Howard Law School became the first team representing a historically Black college to do so. That young lady is now an Assistant Federal Public Defender.

The first college trip taken by the foundation was significant in many ways. That trip included two young baseball teams that played while also having the opportunity to visit and experience college campuses. One of the players later joined our college bound program and went on to attend a leading liberal arts college in Ohio where he became the first Black student to be elected president of a major student organization. After completing a graduate degree in New York, he spent three years as a resident director at the University of Illinois; six years as an assistant director for residence life at Ohio State University and is now an associate director for residence life at Virginia Tech University.

What happens to the future of a promising student who becomes pregnant at the age of sixteen? One of our top students attending a high academic parochial school faced that challenge. An excellent support team that included a supportive family helped the young lady graduate from high school on time. She went on to Illinois State University with her child and graduated with a double major. The child who was raised on a college campus later was accepted to that same college after graduating from high school.

A brilliant young lady from a high academic parochial high school joined our group a little after her boyfriend joined. He was a basketball player, and she was a cheerleader. Her grades and test scores demonstrated that she was on track for success and did not need us, but she became an inspiration to her peers and younger students. She tutored and encouraged other students and one day came to me for advice on where she should go to college.

What do you tell a student who can practically go anywhere in the country on an academic scholarship? As she investigated schools she was leaning towards a little school in Iowa called Grinnell College – an elite yet relatively unknown school. The interesting thing was that I was trying to convince her best friend to consider Drake University in Iowa. The question I was constantly asked, "IOWA"??? Followed by, "Do they have Black people in Iowa"??? She mentioned to her high school counselor that she was considering Drake University and was told that Drake is a competitive school and that she needed to focus on schools she could gain acceptance. I asked her if she believed in herself and she said yes. Both young ladies ended up in Iowa with one at Drake and the other at Grinnell. Both graduated with one continuing her education and graduating from law school while the other finished a master's degree before being named Interim Chief Communications Officer at the City of Des Moines. She also went on to co-found "Back 2 School Bash / Back to School Iowa" a nonprofit assisting Iowa students – as well as serve for over eight years as a mentor for Mentor Iowa.

One of my lowest points with the organization was when I convinced a young lady to attend a school she did not want to attend

– which she received a full scholarship for four years – instead of attempting to attend a school that she wanted to attend, but her mother could not afford. I remember the day she said in anger, "I hope I never see you again." I did not hear from her for years and hoped that I did not ruin her life. I later heard that she was doing great and had even started a dance group at the school, but I still never heard from her. One day while shopping at a grocery store in my neighborhood, a woman ran up to me and hugged me. It was that young lady. She told me that she had graduated from the University in less than four years and was hired by a large company in a management position. She had purchased a house in my neighborhood. She said she wanted to contact me for a long time but was too embarrassed after the way she last spoke to me. She hugged me and said thank you for not listening to a stubborn young girl.

Success stories for the foundation grew in number each year. We began to receive numerous grants and were honored as one of the top funded organizations by the Springboard Foundation. I accepted the award and gave a speech at the Springboard Foundation award dinner about our foundation and our students. Some students from another organization performed at the dinner and stayed to hear me speak. Afterward, they came to me and said that my students were lucky to be in a program that allowed them to visit colleges across the country. I asked them what colleges they had visited and they told me only the ones in Chicago. They were from the Sudan and were excited about the opportunity to be in the United States. I told them my organization was about to take a college trip to New Orleans and they were welcome to join us at no expense to them or their chaperones. I received a huge hug from a group of very happy kids. They were able to join us on our college trip to New Orleans, and they had the time of their lives. One of the students called me later that year after receiving a full scholarship to college.

People often asked why our college bound students were not allowed to vote for their officers. I appointed each officer based on their contributions to the organization and academic performance. Officers were announced at each annual graduation dinner during a special candlelit ceremony – later changed to a rose ceremony – where the current officers would pass a candle to the newly appointed officer. Being president was taken seriously by all students, and one day a young man attending a trip with us to the Wisconsin Dells found out. The young man was a guest of one of our students and became loud while throwing things at people on the bus. One father who attended the trip as a chaperone asked me if I needed him to straighten the young man out and I just smiled and said, "trust me, it will be okay in a minute." The young man reached back to throw an object and was stopped by the student president. She introduced herself, informed him that his behavior was unacceptable and would not be tolerated. Before he could respond, she laid down the law. The young man made the mistake of rising from his seat when every young man in the organization stood and told him, "do not disrespect our president." As the young man sat back in his seat, the father looked at me and said, "tough little cookie isn't she?" That young lady went on to graduate with an engineering degree from Purdue University.

Our students were always encouraged to plan for their future continuously. Many used part time jobs to help save for college. One student was determined to save enough money for college to avoid placing a strain on his family. He had a part time job and bought himself a car to get to school and work. One snowy Chicago night the city snowplows were clearing the neighborhood streets. His car was parked in front of his house when a snow plow shovel ripped into the side of his vehicle. He heard the screeching of metal on metal and looked out the window and saw his car being torn apart by the snow plow. He ran out into the snow and tried to catch up with the snow plow, but there was too much snow, and it was much too cold to be outdoors. He looked at his car in disbelief.

The next day he called the city to report the incident but since he did not see the snow plow's license plate they told him there was no proof the snow plow belonged to the city. He wondered how many big blue snow plows were driving through Chicago at night that did not belong to the city. He gave up and decided to use the passenger door to get in the car and drive it as long as he could.

When I found out what happened, I wrote a letter to his city councilman explaining that I could personally check city records of snow plowing in the neighborhoods and get the schedule for the night the young man's car was damaged. I asked if she wanted to handle the situation or if she wanted me to do it. The next day the young man was called to the principal office over the classroom intercom. He was worried as his teacher and classmates wondered what he had done. The principal informed him he had a call from the city councilman and needed to meet with her. The councilman took estimates to fix the young man's car and he was eventually issued a check for the damage. That young man went on to major in electrical engineering and graduate from Southern Illinois University in Carbondale.

That was a tough year in the city for young men who dared to succeed. We had a young man in our group who was awarded a full academic scholarship to college. He had become depressed with a lot of things going on in his personal life and missed some assignments in a history class. His teacher informed him that he would receive an F no matter how he did on the final exam and would lose the scholarship he was awarded. This was a teacher who dressed in African attire, wore the wooden medallions and regularly spoke of Black Power. Now he was willing to cause a young Black male to lose a full scholarship to teach him a lesson.

The principal of that high school loved his students. When he heard about the situation he called a meeting of the teacher, student and parents. He began the meeting with, "we need to come to an agreement that will be in the best interest of the student." He then asked the teacher if he could give the young man extra work to make up for the missed assignments and allow his final exam to dictate his fate. The teacher sat back in his seat with his arms crossed and said no. He went on to inform the principal that no one can dictate what happens in his class and he would contact the union if the principal tried to make him do anything. The principal looked at the teacher and smiled. He told him he was by no means threatening him. He told the teacher to do what he felt was best. Then he said he planned to do what he felt was best the following year when selecting staff that he felt could best prepare his students. The teacher asked if that was a threat and the principal said no but that no one could tell him how to run his school. He asked the teacher if he understood. The young man was given extra assignments which he completed as well as passed the final exam. That young man went on to receive the scholarship, graduate from college as well as serve his nation while fighting with the U.S. Army in Iraq. That young man was my son.

12

A TIME FOR CELEBRITIES

People Magazine and AOL started an e-mentoring program called the Digital Hero Program and selected programs from the PowerUp program to assign celebrity mentors. The program matched students with celebrities based on personal profiles (consisting of individual likes, dislikes and interest) to communicate via email. Our program was selected to participate.

One of our students had been accepted to Princeton University and her profile was an excellent match for the owner of some of the most successful restaurants in New York. The only problem was the restaurant owner was a male and the student was a female – the program only matched mentors and mentees of the same gender. After a discussion with the young lady's parents the two were allowed to be matched. Their relationship grew and she was flown into New York with the head of our mentoring program to meet her mentor and eat at his restaurants. The young lady went on to graduate from Princeton University and finish her graduate work at Duke University.

Another student was matched with the head of a record label and clothing line. His goal was a career in entertainment and his mentor provided him with an internship after his senior year of high school in New York. That young man went on to graduate from Morehouse College.

One actor/tap dancer requested to be matched with our most challenging student. Once again we found a student of the opposite gender. She was not a challenging young lady as much as a quiet young lady who stayed to herself. The two of them communicated often until he passed away.

The e-mentoring program was well planned out and consisted of many safeguards. It was designed and headed by a woman who worked with the White House on the development of standards in mentoring programs. The students were so excited about the program that they invited the President of People magazine and the designer of the mentoring program to be acknowledged at their annual graduation dinner – both accepted and attended. It was amazing when the head of the mentoring program spoke and informed the audience that of all her many accomplishments in her lifetime, this was the first time that she had ever been honored. She thanked the students and organization for the honor, and few years after the dinner, we later found out that she passed away.

It was a surprising day in the neighborhood when the president of People Magazine showed up at our office in a limo to meet our students. One student told me, "Somebody is lost out there in a limo". Out of the limo stepped a woman with no fear of the neighborhood with a big smile and hug for everyone.

The Digital Hero program eventually ended but we continued a virtual mentoring program matching our high school students with our former students who had graduated from college – as well as young professionals throughout the country. Those relationships blossomed and one young lady ended up singing at her mentor's wedding.

One day while reading an article about a former Chicago high school student who had become a NFL player, I noticed he was holding a free football clinic at the park where our college bound group met. I never really reached out to professional athletes since my focus was on academics. But this athlete happened to be a graduate of Whitney Young high school (the top academic school in the city). Further research on this player revealed that he was inducted into the University of Miami Iron Arrow Honor Society – the highest honor bestowed by the university. This young man was much more than an athlete!

The article had a phone number to get more information about the football clinic and led me to meeting his father (the executive director for his foundation). We got together and discussed his foundation and mine to find common synergies. We established a relationship and I later became a board member of his foundation and met some of the most amazing people – which included many educators. The young ladies in our group were invited to be hostesses at his annual scholarship dinner where they escorted professional football players into the room. The head of our mentoring program supervised the hostesses while each hostess never forgot their day with the pros.

Our relationship grew and we worked together to host a college fair in a local indoor shopping mall (Evergreen Plaza). The fair helped us develop yet another connection with the mall management team. The player was not able to attend the fair so he had a video recorded welcoming students and colleges to the fair that we played on a loop until the fair ended. The great thing about him was how genuinely sincere he was in helping others. Each year his foundation supported our graduation dinner and also helped provide scholarships for some of our students.

13

CLOSING TIME

In 2008 the fall of the financial markets resulted in reduced and lost grants for many nonprofits. Make A Difference had grown to high school and elementary school programs for students throughout the city. I had lost my job and had to move to another state where I could find work and the grants for the foundation began to disappear. We decided to close both locations and shut down all programs.

It had been a tremendous run for over 20 years with every student being accepted into college and approximately seventy percent receiving college degrees. Graduates from the program were doctors, lawyers, educators, engineers, accountants and professionals throughout the country. But we all had to meet one final evening to empty the offices and close for the last time. Students packed up things for storage as they reminisced on the years gone past. When the last box was packed and loaded on the truck, we all sat together and reminisced. A final hug and off we went in different directions as the end had finally arrived.